A Cluster

Of Lights

Copyright © Michael Pitman 2017

ISBN 978-0-9930067-1-5

A catalogue record for this book is available from the British Library.

The right of Michael Pitman to be identified as the Author of this Work has been asserted by him in accordance with the Copyright, Designs and Patents Act 1988.

All Rights Reserved. Apart from any use expressly permitted under UK copyright law no part of this publication may be reproduced, stored in an alternative retrieval system to the one purchased or transmitted in any form or by any means electronic, mechanical, photocopying, recording or otherwise without the prior permission in writing of the Author.

Published by Merops Press

Websites:
www.scienceandphilosophy.co.uk
www.cosmicconnections.co.uk
www.michaelpitmanbooks.co.uk
www.scienceandthesoul.co.uk

Acknowledgements: Suzanne, my wife, Marianne, Emmanuel and Françoise.

Contents

Introduction *5*
What pleasure *6*
Spring curls in *7*
Out of Steam (1968) *7*
Welsh Stream (1963) *8*
The Nature of Polarity *10*
Flamenco *11*
Flakes of Fire *12*
The forest like a galleon sways *13*
Across a salt marsh... .... *13*
Song at the Tomb of Pir Suleiman (1970) .. *14*
A Dance on Helicon (1966) *16*
In bouncing sharps and flats *17*
Sunshine tiptoed softly *18*
Green Sybil *19*
Tintagel *20*
Switched off....switched on *21*
Where the deep sky folds *24*
What's for Real? *25*
Cadbury Castle (1975) *26*
Sunday Walk *27*
Metamorphosis *28*
I ran, ran like taking off *29*
Love's Conceit (à Watteau) *30*
Golden and white *31*

Nereus' Passionate Sea (1965) 32
Elysian Ache 35
Parting Silence Shared Apart 36
I had placed you 36
Out of a single glance 37
Muffled up 37
The Touch of a Master Man (1958) 38
Ancient Greece (1962) 39
Addison's Walk (1966) 41
Murree (1970) 42
Man, thinking, makes a fool of God 43
Winds of consciousness 43
Techno-city 44
Come close! The bow is flexed 45
Beneath the radiant canopy 45
Benediction and the curse 46
Sound, Light, Ocean. 46
I pondered earth from inner space 47
Breakthrough 47
A child of the starry heaven 48
Bells at Trumpington Church 48
The Call 49
On a Broadcast Live from Mir (Peace) 50

Introduction

Poetry is evocative and subjective. One man's meat may be another's poison or, at best, arouse indifference. Just as individual tastes differ so, from culture to culture and time to time, do styles of expression, popular themes and the imagery of verse.

Nor is a poem rational in the way of logic or objective science. Nevertheless its artistry is not irrational. Every work of art evokes, which is its essence, feeling. To this end a poem's arrangement sometimes involves rhythmic format and rhyme while at others the lyric is looser and less orderly. Always, however, a compressed spring of words propels the reader to a flight of understanding, universal principle and quickening imagination.

Whether this book is called A Cluster of Lights, A String of Pearls or A Casket of Jewels is immaterial. Its sparkles were mostly written between 1965 and 1975; and I hope that one, several or even all of them give you pleasure.

What pleasure just to bask
   in ancient tree-light, Puck-like
propped against a trunk beneath the boughs
   that sway this forest family!
Towers of years; the wind is soughing
   as it has each moment of
   an ageless history of time!

   Aren't I in Eden here?

Death's free-fallen through the winter
   into spring. From the temporary
graveyard green-fire rises like a phoenix -
   buds and sprigs that thrust, spin, wriggle
winging fresh-born, burning out
   into the coloured air.
   Quiet contemplation dives

   into a pool of thought.

Thousand-fold a miracle, each leaf
   printed onto space is a real
and three-dimensional kind of dream.
   What Mind linked light and life like this
and realised green galaxies,
   a million stars with arms upraised
   in worship of their Sun?

   Into an ocean gently

swims the stream of life, seasons dancing
   like the Graces in a ring.
The start's the end, the end's the start,
   neither in the flux is either
but a pulse, a Buddhist paradox,
   endless glistening answers

   fluttering in a virtual breeze.

Spring curls in on a south-westerly
    drumming, billowing, blasting with leaf.
It whistles 'go!' in winter's ear,
    unfurls its colours, strikes a march
and storms the world with birth-rain.
    Free! Jaunty water winks once more,
spring's eye's nubile, spring's heart's warm,
    spring's quivering, glad to be born
and brim towards crescendos of
    the golden music summer scores.

Out of Steam (1968)

The weather echoes through our brain
    tapping in code that our engine's
been passed into memory line.
    The signal is level, the siding's
a motionless pride of old men.
    Fire was our power, in the flux
of our hour from the heart white blood
    flew, stung the rod, pummelled motion
to rhythm that roared out alive,
    that rammed home the message, the warmth
and the fury, the grandeur of steam.
    That journey's done, this station's
unscheduled, its buffer dead-ended.
    Rust after rain, the nettles, just
one appointment with the Guv'nor,
    expressly nowhere but the Yard.

Welsh Stream (1963)

Collapse
  off the bald,
    bright stones
      in rough gushes clatters down
      off a hundred brinks round
      the hills. A thousand catches sing

blown off the water, shook off the stream;
rings throb and shake and light globes
pulse away across like folds on folds
in sablest, thickest velveteen

see, wink, wade over, fade and die.
The pan of sun shifts wirelight
live, electric, swashing and crashing,
bubbling gold-laced lapped on firewater

many, many dancing, wincing
forks of lightning in a liquid storm.
Rings quake, radiate, plash, bide,
part, consummate in sheets again, ride

off in water-nets, always leaving. Here
dart flame and flare held off the mad sky
in shredded light; and the treadling rush
of sapphire trinket water gushes

like hordes unleashed hysterically.
Water-plough, water-furrow; look up,
up, look, thrummed down at this pail
of rock high water winched off the skyrail

flocks of spray where the lean rowan
clutches out at air. Sheer from that wispish
bough the spring has threshed through
fifty feet or more and hurled heavy

water splattering this scoured dish
wherein it roars like corrie wind
around whose brimming rim thin
overlaps are skimmed and hurdled

down a bouldered course of foam.
Swirling, curling, scooped and swept
along a cataract of water
frolic of a silver laughter

joshed and playful, shot towards the sea.
Wheel of the weather, round and round
the rain; shadows boom and this welsh cwm
strews mountains-full of heaven to ground!

The Nature of Polarity

Female to male you polarise,
   you magnetise me to the fingertips.
Each to each, antennae pulse
   and with increasing frequency flip
to and fro in those half-conscious tests
   that bodies meeting always make.
In each of us acceptance magnifies
   until a fruit of fever sweats.
What is Eve's apple but her play?
   Eyes enkindled sparkle with
a flame as supple as the movements
   that surround an invitation
beamed from deep in femininity.
   Yes! Apple, mango, grape and every
luscious, heady shape of juice in one.
   A million nerves like leaves
are fluttering in the rising gale.
   A tug of lust, rope a-quiver;
in drawing drawn the muscles
   of our minds were locking into
harmony; hearts, hands and lips were sliding
   to a kiss that threw the words away.

Flamenco.

O the murmuring ferns in your humming
    O the moons in your fingertips
and roses pressed from off your lips -
    a rising slight excitement is
    smouldering promise of a bliss.

In frills and circles of the water
    wind skirmishes like restless blood
and hunts like a gypsy guitar -
    the rising strings of a glance are
    keen to the touch of hands of power.

There is no question, fire has broken out.
    Roll back the clouds, the horses fly
O archèd pride and strength of sigh -
    a rising flower of night is burst
    beneath the trampling hooves of love.

Flakes of Fire

The sky is bruised. Exhausted purple,
   red and gold illuminate
no more than silhouettes and shades.
   At summer's rim this broken fire
is crowning death - royal cremation
   up against the twilight, sunset's wild throes
   till darkness claims the ashes of the year.

A spirit haunts the autumn, misty as
   a time of passing, shuffling up the leaves
like embers to a blaze of memories.
   An impossible love, nostalgia is
aching to the fingertips and he
   lives deep in feeling that would die
   O hungry to the universal sky!

The forest like a galleon sways
   and roars with wind in seas of leaves
proclaiming from the highest mast
   its glorious spring. Storms of birth
have burst in every quarter,
   buds are bouncing with that laughter
countless as the sparkling water
   of swashbuckling, swelling May.

Ship of the world, the four winds blow;
   Mother stands, inspiring, at the prow
and, as her rippling garments flow,
   she rides sap's tide into a wake
of blossom, song and fruitfulness
   regaling us towards harvest home.

Across a salt marsh...

Imperial sea has swept flat
   the land and wind flung up
a wide and empty atmosphere.
   The elements commingle and reflect
each other in a stream of time.
   Lights are moistened, shadows smudged,
blurred the changing watercolours
   of the Artist's wash. Buoyant strokes,
a sharp hawk flaps and navigates.
   Wheeling hours immerse the city,
aeons rinse its calculations
   in an ocean of the natural mind.

Song at the Tomb of Pir Suleiman (1970)

A *Pir* (pronounced 'peer') is a muslim holy man. Suleiman's tomb is situated in a small park on the Shalimar side of Lahore near the freight marshalling yards. Ragged flags like pennants flutter round and by night it is lit with many small earthenware lamps. The *Mir'aj* of the Prophet Mohammed was the inner mystic experience of the flight of his soul. *Haj* is pilgrimage to Mecca.

    At dawn the crier from his tower
        calls till the darkness has dissolved.
    The shadows die. A crescent sun's
        expanding from a wall-less tomb

    and, brilliantly, the soul of Day
        eliminates its mortal night.
    If dying born, then Suleiman
        was swift as light into the dance

    of multitudes who on the winds
        of inner sky fly high and higher –
    he must still be rising right
        inside the songs of paradise.

    Waves of prayer propel his *mi'raj*
        surfing towards an endless shore,
    Suleiman is heaven-riding
        like Mohammed past the stars

    into expanding haloes of the heart,
        pirouetting up in streams
    and bursting to the angel lights
        on wings of whirling flame.

From centre after centre flow
    the radiant forms his love desires,
intense attention, rapt devotion
    that the mystic path inspires.

Gaze on, wild traveller, watch
    with natural velocity
cinematic shows of thought
    upon the screen's infinity.

Gaze on until you're eased up
    absolutely out of mind
on the real *haj* to the seventh heaven
    of Rajah, Allah, the Divine.

A Dance on Helicon (1966)

(Helicon is a Greek mountain in whose groves and valleys
the nine Muses, spirits of the arts, are said to dwell).

        Apollo's president. Around
           his altar atmospheric charges
    fluctuate like essences of song.
        Here leave limbo, snap into
    the instant heart of time that's music,
        godlike ride each age at once,
           come burst into creation's breeze.

Take drum, take cymbal, muscularly
    arouse the fabric of a feeling,
invoke the Muses to this astral air.
    Shaking bass roves like a phantom
woven in the texture of the place
    like an impelling, edgeless nerve
    about the insubstantial grove.

Piano flies like water over stones.
    Each baton stroke's a celebrant,
a priest who taps the mysteries
    and floods them out of unseen sources
ranged behind the end of space.
    Release their rhythms, free me too
    and prove the Orphean dance is true.

Stronger now, the river of the band
    is rising. On the surface words
are cast in flights of ripples driven
    under streaming blasts of air; reason
is dissolving deeper in the tide
    where drowning we are born(e), each one,
    into a Muse's vibrant arms.

Sound's aurora trembles, lights dance
    from her eyes and every move
is moving closer, every touch
    from fingertip to lip in love
is harmonised as we ascend
    into the garden of the gods,
    into the heights called Helicon.

In bouncing sharps and flats of breeze
    slung lightly as a melody
between the rattling, careless leaves
    a net of spider's spun. No fret,
no chord, an interlude of silence...
    Struggling strings! At a stroke a riff,

a rush of bliss, a flickering
    refrain until the flutter dies.
Beneath the stars, between the dews
    and sunshine blown about by wind,
in tactic, tempo and intent
    here just a spider calls the tune.

Sunshine tiptoed softly dripping
    bliss in every line: I tripped
down to the pool with the tree-light
    in my eyes, I drifted like a smoke
and drifted other wise, so fine!
    A swimming logic in my mind!

And there about the noon, dear cool,
    I got baptised in Arden pool,
the fire grew higher and the sunshine
    lifted lightly to still finer
volume till I knew the golden rule -
    knowing little much a kinder fool!

So come, I only want you
    knowing this, that sunshine softly
in your head is, little do you
    know it, here in mine: and here in mine
is melting like a snowflake
    past the holy edge of time.

Green Sybil

Before the hurricanes of leaf
   and golden winds of autumn stood she -
a wisp of summer still but clouds
   of rock above the girl foretold
a dream, her pale red hair spun in
   the breezes of a prophecy.

Within her crystal gaze a film
   of destiny unwound, a future
war of men and gods - silence
   cast broad her thought as clear as words.
"Benighted sense and science, turn
   from greed, refrain from arrogance

towards Earth, whose body is your own.
   A black wind blows, the more it knows
the more its reasons decompose
   the natural songs of sap and blood.
You steal the womb; do you forget
   the shadows of this rape are yours?

And death. Do you know desolation?
   You may be clever but not wise,
refrain from war, save all the sighs
   that from assault on Mother rise.
Now, while I gong the knell of night
   don't choose winter and the grave."

Tintagel

I meditate as Celtic monk
    called to his Lord on this prow'd
precipice. Sun, ocean, thunder
    are a natural magic ages young
    that bind Tintagel to my heart.

Huge slabs of time locked in the cliffs
    diminish me without a word
to the point of silence that expands into
    a timeless, town-less history
    and the spirit of this place.

White centuries of surf have boomed,
    insistent breakers wash and flush
away the cloud of thought called mind;
    above, grey gulls swing screaming on
    a roller-coaster of a gale.

Around the cliff-top congregate
    a church and tombs of local souls
who in a twinkling like sea-glitter
    bubbled, frothed and, nearly nothing
    in a great age, burst away. I'll

join them when I sail, Pendragon,
    at the hour of passing over
my horizon, an adventure through
    full-blooded sundown and the golden
    harbour-gates of Avalon.

Switched off….switched on

I switched off the motor,
   got out, clunked the door shut...
silence in the wide world.

Chains of bobbing shadow fly
   o'er bouncy hedge and swaying trees,
down marches of field an atlas
   of the sun and cloud is blown.

Pennant of the life spirit,
   dog-trot and whim of the green wind,
fluttering drums of rain again
   where hours without horizon wag.

No leash! No dead-line anywhere
   except the blood of autumn,
fallen leaves! Another clock, hands off,
   a race as fast as sunlight strives!

Where man ends God begins, vast art
   of sky and royal air above
these furrowed seas and waves of grass.
   A hedgerow scintillates with finch

and oxygen is fresh to drink;
   drink deep and hitch a molecule
to hike imagination into roots
   through lung down blood to cell-fire

closer than breathing, everywhere!
   Refreshment and renewal.
A silent sphere of industry,
   the flywheels whirr, gears and presses

purr, no care, and banking's here,
   starchy business and biochemistry
in every pore of every day
   inside the gyroscopic year.

Next to nothing, just a smudge of power
   on space cements the world together,
in-and-out-of-being flight
   of the electron constitutes

spark and glue in every field of
   life and its activities!
Each leaf's a battery wired lightly
   to the sun, photoelectric plant

of some bionic circuit strung
   between us and the stars; from sun
through leaf my lamp is lit.
   Transparent texture, trinity,

from water, light and air a shoot
   matures into the blessing of
our daily bread; from kiss of cosmos
   sap is transformed into blood.

As male and female interlock
   leaves are wholly interlocked with us,
plant with creature's intertwined.
   I bank on light's green funds, the cash

each muscle draws for motion flows
   from harvest-time. Life's engine purrs,
reactions ripple down their freeways
   driven by a haloed star.

Rare reactivity! Whose patterns stream
    like symphonies, each electronic
note correct, every programmed step
    charged with intent - from pure light life.

I've tumbled on a sunbeam down
    through nature's doors, I've roved half
round the universe yet only gazed
    in space of mind, majestic focus

fielded from a throne of grass.
    I climbed aboard a rolling cloud
of happiness, breathed back the kiss
    soft as a silver man alone in this.

Where the deep sky folds (1962)

Where the deep sky folds
  and the hawthorn blows
here live I. Summers
  and winters pass me by.
I whistle the wind
hear the first bird call
  hear the red leaf fall
  and the roar of the rain.

I smile and I flower
  in that shining hour
of the sun. Autumn
  and spring, all the run
of the wild I dream
like a child content
  wrapped in the blanket
  of the firmament.

What's for Real?

A dab hand at nothing
  the Chinese artist whisks
reed, red wind and lines
  of mountains from the mist.

Can't catch a mood except
  in mind; the poet flips
a palette of phantoms
  into the fifth dimension.

A musician brushes sound
  on silence; at his signal
from thin air the colours
  of a song appear.

Inspiration conjures something
  out of nothing. Are creations
realised in mind a copy
  of the real mystery?

Cadbury Castle (1975)

Sweet smell of ages, lichens, leaves,
   years, tombs and only wild-life here.
Now in deep country underneath
   the royal air and vast art of clouds
modernity is dwindled to a speck,
   its stress dissolved into a spotless
wind of cool, transparent air.
   We are Arthurs, this is Camelot;

although its walls are lost in banks
   of evening and its busy halls entombed
in grass, a spirit sings in silence
   and our hearts are lifted towards
the sunset. Golden, blood-red, purple
   lights are gathering in the west,

all eyes are drawn to the port of death -
   quests, grails and magic rings that pass
you through to everlasting life in Avalon.
   Underneath the spray of evening stars
can you grasp a shady outline
   of the legend and his friends at table?
Can you see the ghosts of heroes
   up against the darkness battling

with ideals of radiance and truth?
   Although the dream's suspended
on a cusp of summer moon,
   it seems as if the grail has banished
shadows and its inner sun
   illuminates the knights' communion.

Sunday Walk

We trod the freshening hilltops high
   along an amazing, flying sky,
we trod the air, we trod the line
   into a new view of our minds.

Wind dances past a-jig with grass
   of track which, fading, loses track...
a walking pace and singing space
   are in the arms of laughter.

Life with these clouds, where hair flies wild
   like turbans in Afghanistan,
where sunshine pours through showers of tears
   I felt us coming home again.

Beneath the tumbling sky we lay,
   beneath the purples piled like mountains,
poetry as clear as air where
   couched like your king on adiantum fern

I loved our passage through the world.
   We loved so well from every pore
that, praising life, if death had called
   I'd just have gone, not begged for more.

Short the week-end, short the life
   we pass like weather in time's sky,
shapes of mind, moods of cloud or smiles
   that, currents in us, make us shine.

A clear and careless sky's the summer
   of the soul. As, dying, we
review the weather of our life
   the truth is, as our friends remember,

very little's more important
   than the laughter! Whence we gravitated
gently down our mindscape
   to the chits and chores of Monday.

Metamorphosis

Where boughs of leaves sway like the sea
   and tulips rollick endlessly
into that cataract of energy, the wind,
   on tip-toe did I swim.

It's flood today, no other way
   so fine - like surf the roar of firs
and spirits of the flowers press
   kisses to the loose, spring air.

O sweet a shower, strings of sitar,
   sweet swims this fish in streams
of love-fed fire, sweet lit this lamp
   wired lightly to the sun.

The flood-light glows, at once I know
   any parts that do not flow
trouble in a neighbour's mind-space
   that we need to melt to go.

This chrysalis of dawning's split
   to such a birth of wonder
that I scarcely care to speak
   as I am born to fly…

I ran, ran like taking off,
   never did the breathless ease
run out. It is a pouch of fire,
   this head, conceiving me
   about the unearth universe!

How the grass flows! Quicksilver
   I, with knowledge like a god's, keen
to the turning prism of events
   recline on cushions of the mind.
   This is a kingship full alive!

Alive! Switched on with powerful,
   peaceful lens! All that's outside's
inside, I'm a screen of changing moods
   and lights of day, a royal, rich
   union with sunshine and the land.

Not just a screen! From deep in thought
   a golden alchemy transmutes
base sense into a time-free world
   of purpose, principle and plan,
   the archetypes of universal mind.

Sharper than a laser, finer
   than the atom's heart and deeper
than the boundaries of space
   you dive and there may start to feel
   the radiance of his Lordship's face.

Love's Conceit (à Watteau)

I love to look, I look to love
  the dream that flatters self-deceit.
Silver satin in Parisian parks?
  A model deep beneath the elms
strikes airs - O Ma'amselle, I admire
  you who've struck a made-to-measure
seam, illusion of love's treasured self.
  The idyll's filmed, the beauty glossed
into a fop of feeling, one
  with Narcissus quite complete.
She prances, fades, ho, *sans un mot*
  into the brushwork of the trees.

I created, like spilt music,
  moods entwined in tenderness
until my warm blood broke like stars.
  I modelled you inside the fashion
of a fire-eyed melancholy,
  dressed you up and photographed you
in my heart's eye's precious light.
  A dream come true's no dream; it's true
I loved romance more than loved you.
  Here, where you couldn't enter in,
you left a heart enshrined which died
  the death of my ideal's conceit.

Golden and white, the lights of a hymn.
    Above the altar in a brilliant
clasp of time the praying hands
    and symmetry of stained-glass window

arch towards an endless firmament
    that, at the same time, they enclose. Radiant
shadows of the saints enshrine the light
    which lights all bodies from within.

From silence sound, from stillness stream,
    creation's stream in which we dream
issues like a film from peace.
    Rend time's fabric, you will see

time is motion's second nature,
    waves of nothing rolled to something
for a moment in the Great Game
    overlapping pure infinity.

Past and future ghost the present,
    shadows flutter round the essence -
in the chancel on the altar
    coolness of the candlelight remains.

I'd take the mystic life for real,
    light up my darkness, crack my tomb
and cloak me in a master-peace
    of knowledge spun on wheels of prayer.

Sanctify me, lift me past
    the calculations of my brain,
make the Point where our relationship's
    transformed into Communion.

Nereus' Passionate Sea (1965)

I would restrain the high and troubled tide
   and press it to my saddening breast
but it lies wide
   and I must rest.
Caves murmur round a hungry song,
   the dim waves running chafe and throng.

Rolling worlds and clouds of water,
   which were my kingdom, with pale weight
and dark laughter
   wildly execrate.
Caves percolate a restless song,
   currents rip and race along.

Once I willed or even willed them not,
   the waves obeyed; but now my charge
by gods endowed
   has grown too strong.
Caves swirl with a rising song
   as threatening as loud.

I, Nereus, have grown old. Weakly I lean
   upon this golden trident and the arm
of Doris, queen
   of calm profundities.
Caves shudder with unbridled rushes
   as white horses crash asunder.

I know not, no, nor understand
   the boundaries of fury's flow;
at the far strand
   anger inundates the land.
Caves echo with a thunderous boom
   of war and doom.

Blind swell and seething billow
    strew the fate of ships like leaves;
sea-forms are driven
    on the cataract of storm.
Caves moan with devil winds,
    rocks thud with pouring bulk.

I have drawn my daughters fifty
    down to the beryl caverns deep,
down from the wilful sky
    and the surface sweep.
Caves spout and drench with spray
    like roaring battle-day.

Where they played upon the wake
    black wind has bundled clouds
and bitter flakes
    whirl from the shroud.
Caves at the shore or coral deep
    both by now deny retreat.

Master-less, run wild, the sullen
    sudden waves and sky
combine to threaten
    death and chaos nigh.
Caves once were home
    but home is washed away.

Waves pound, surges mutter,
    eye of cyclone spins the clutter
of a kingdom
    now in disarray.
Caves, once a refuge, now expel
    this royal refugee.

I would shrink such chaos
   to the compass of my arms,
I would care for rampant Ocean
   stroking down despair.
Cool caves were courts
   whence used to issue care.

Despair! A main of tumult
   in my mind! And yet a titan
in demesne needs only will
   to find the power to solve the pain.
I will up and summon
   all the elements from open sea.

Whites of wild eyes, screams of lament
   have whipped a hurricane
whose salty trail is tears of grief.
   O, let order's banner be unfurled;
may some reviving anthem
   ravel up demonic anarchy.

I call. I cry. I am not heard.
   Nets of turbulence entangle,
shocks hurl, confusion spins me -
   though immortal I would die.
Therefore, once life's spuming fret
   has settled, find where I might lie.

Then, Leukothea, wrap me
   in a blanket made of waves
and drop me gently to a deep
   and golden grave.
Such shrine, I swear, will only resonate
   with oceanic hymns of praise.

Elysian Ache

The old were upstairs floating down,
   the middle ages trying to hang on
the young came under like a bomb.

   I want to lift off, hard to freeze
I want the deep sun in my eyes
   and wrinkles smiling sure as wise,

an edge as keen as fire on time
   that burns me into elfinhood.
O weight of universities,
   don't you feel too much fact's disease?

Orpheus with stupendous alchemy
   forged tensile strings of poesy -
the chords drift slack in verbose rain

   we're hungry for them back again.
Each one of us is born to fly
   hardly speaking lest we lose our high.

It's true! And we'd do anything
   and we do everything to bring
this ache on strong, this wild god driving
   to the fingertips in love.

Solid is shadow, fact is ghost
   and least a ghost who loves the most
and real the dream born in the stream

   of joy - all else is thinking lost.
I left the grave I'd figured in,
   I'm not a body, not that one

that drags me to the city fun.
   Wind blows me light across the grass
things have come to a pretty pass
   loving so much I'd die for less...

Parting Silence Shared Apart

Your lips, my fingertip,
   ways to join our separation.
Diamond lights of seasons
   sparkle round our ring of time.
Pipes of peace, the drums of discontent,
   the turning turned again
until the heart's desire was met,
   all the highlights, loves and songs
now leap from memory
   into nostalgia's maze of our amazing days.

I saw you wave, I watched
   the train of my reality retreat.
The vision of the day was blurred confusion,
   life without you
   really only nonsense.

I had placed you in the dreams
   of walks under avenues
in warm, campion after-rain woods,
   tenderness until you broke
my warm blood out like stars.
   Our hearts were wound together
with a silver twine of flowers
   I picked - a simple link, a ring
that, having run the race of summer,
   still holds my slippery world in place.

Out of a single glance
   that sparkled like snow
under the blue air of winter
   a symphony of love grew.

Out of a quaver on
   your lips, a momentary warmth
that spun the north wind
   into spring, I saw you clearly.

Out of a flirtatious ripple
   through your hair and eyes and everywhere
the smile of care I care for
   rushed me into ecstasy.

Muffled up but inside scattered
   like a leaf in arctic wind,
to my breast you pressed for comfort,
   to the source of turbulence.

Out of drifting chords of rain
   from fragile hearts we tried again
and found our love and gave our truth
   wrapped in warm, light atmosphere.

The Touch of a Master Man (1958)

    Walking off the gangplank
      with long and mighty strides,
    with tarry hands and feet,
      rough voice and ragged clothes,
    with tangled hair and a coarse beard
      a worn and tall and fearless sailor.
    From the street he picked
      an old grey lute, for no-one else
    cared for the thing.
      With pink, plucked strings it was
    all battered with the time and wear.
      And he played, he played
    not like himself, a ragged sailor
      but a melody sweet and clear.
    All stopped and listened
      as he played, for so soothing
    a melody plucked at their hearts
      as the old lute's strings were plucked.
    And they cried for the lute
      by the dockside quay,
    the old, unwanted lute.
      And all by the touch
      of a master man.

Ancient Greece (1962)

Would I were in lands
that curving Grecian vases well portray -
bulls, minotaurs and misty gods,
ragged valleys where the fighting sweat
flows from heroes' backs which gleam like burnished gold
and ache with heavy toil
while brazen sun beats ever down from cloudless skies.
I wish I were at that same army's camp
at eve, where dark brown waters choke ravine,
coolish breeze pipes reed and spiny grass
and heroes' dusky tents enclose
the song of lyre, wine, stinging joy.

Perfumed smoke from charnel houses
spirals slowly to clear air.
Spirits down in darkness sip of blood
and others restless in the echo
flit like bat to find a resting-place,
a grey-stoned tomb.

There beaches white as snow, grains hot,
whose lilting waves wash hero's corpse
lain splayed upon the sand.

And, on the other hand, mountains
where frenzied Bacchus, ivy-crowned,
leads winding, wine-soaked throng
on paths to savage, cloudy ecstasy.
Those frost-tipped caps in cold moon's glow
keep shiver till the reddening wake of dawn.

Here olive groves, long silty-floored,
spring from the fertile plains;
amid the leafy groves, where Naiads play,
stand marbly temples, white and solid,
pillars where old men wring geometry
and, shadow-dappled, wise philosophers
discuss the universe of man.

Slow time these vases stand,
black, *terra cotta*, some cracked,
and fetch a long and watery shadow
for the reader of their hours.

Addison's Walk (1966)

Early about the sanctuaries
  of morning swims the day. Swan and sky
are gentle omens, reflected
  in a smooth and graceful pool.

As light sparkles from revolving crystals
  birdsong flits and glitters
through the leaves. Twenty times the thought
  surrounded me in flight before

it settled logically: "If time's foreshortened
  by attention, could the sharpest cut
illuminate that mystic paradox
  of timeless interest and love?"

An easter arch of blue above,
  ever the water under the swan,
hand cupped in hand and ease in ease
  in sitting I sank to the skies -

in giving thanks and praise you rise.
  Tulips and the water-meadow,
marl half-dry upon the path of reason,
  saturation on the path of love.

Murree (1970)

Murree is a hill station on the Himalayan foothills
in Northern Pakistan

A cold river flows through the trees
  across dark and ragged wings of cloud
around a hilltop village that is
  disappearing into empty night.

Calm dawn, a resurrection of
  the outlines day will detail,
bowls of valley mist that sway
  and vanish into morning.

Life rubs its eyes, day flowers and
  a buzzard spirals steep as mountains
till his soaring majesty is lost
  in the expanding sun's great light.

Man, thinking, makes a fool of God.

A zoo! The mind of man knows
   only bounds. Incarceration
of soft flesh in wireless puzzles.
   Incarceration in academy?
Did reason make a zoo of men
   who snarled and whined and could not run?
Arid is the spirit's muzzle,
   thought paces in its mental cage
turns, turns again in concrete rage
   that tearless weeps enmeshed in twists
and worried weavings of its own
   when life's a lion that roars in love.

God, thinking makes a fool of man!

Winds of consciousness, weather of the head,
   music, biochemical music;
look how nervous fingers of the wind love trees
   and me leaping with their gale today
through moment's leaves, a spirit in the air
   of loving energy.

The cycle of my knowledge gears up to
   its final throw, orgasm of truth
as insubstantial as the edge on fire,
   last gasp before the climax of the choir –
round and around in wanting nothing I
   grasp facts to let them fly.

Techno-city is a phoenix' pyre;
   as I walked out the bird in me
was rising higher. Philosopher in
   white coat, I disagree that science
sees much inner Me. It feels I've
   hardly been away but long ago
this wind shook out all facts and I
   shone free. No figures in this glow!

Go slow, go fast, come reason light
   and slip the falling town just right,
from out the ashes of man's thought
   wrap through me in this golden fire.
A pantheon of angels rise,
   enchanted hearts, enchanting eyes
and grant me skipping just in time
   to always laugh and love in rhyme.

O make it beauty, make it more
   out of everlasting thunder
tosses and sighs of love-met eyes
   I want the star that never dies:
beyond the parallels of time
   I want just one, one Midnight Sun
to break out into lucid skies
   as pummelling wings begin to rise.

Come close! The bow is flexed,
    its vibrant string lets arrows
that are glances fly, whose tips
    release a flood of energy!
Reciprocal the love-shot, twice
    the resonance, sparkling exchange
as irresistible as gravity,
    immeasurable as musicals

whirls and whirls us in a dance
    as large as space and close as breath.
Two halves made whole in love's embrace
    embrace their state of origin,
seal with an archetypal kiss
    whole human being in a godlike bliss.

Beneath the radiant canopy
    of space a kiss, a naked kiss,
a supernova in the universe
    of love. A union of stars,
a vortex into which are whirled
    the atoms, suns and galaxies,
time's change and all our days until
    alone in heaven at the height
of love-lit night, just right, our peace
    reverberates with cosmic bliss.

Benediction and the curse
   dissolve, mind's laser melts The Book
into an ancient, page-less presence.
   Waves of our turmoil ebb into
a pool of peace, knowledge gathers
   to a web of understanding
union is the realm of paradise
   and we've become its velvet sigh.

Orchestras of hymn break
   onto landscapes of eternal feeling
risen out of reach of words. Grand hours!
   The voice is thrown back and sun streams
through the chords. I'm sound, I shimmer
   in expanding rings through space,
I'm flying to a peak that's angels
   losing everything in light.

Sound, Light, Ocean.

Insistent swells of rock 'n' rhythm
   pump the veins of devotees,
rollers moving in communion,
   seas that run like blood in summer
high. A tide of harmony
   sways up into a crest, unrolls
and vortices of power plunge
   off after into waves of wind,

into the guitar spray a-wing,
   into the breakers of our hearts.
Music's muscle, chariot and
   god-like rider irresistibly combine
to pound the world of cares to foam
   and boom beyond the shores of time.

Is there a quintessential state
  where metaphors evaporate
and leave a golden drop of God?
  I pondered earth from inner space
with us as drifts of light and shapes
  of time hardly more important
than a smile. No matter! Smiles transmute
  life's leaden load to energy!

How obvious the alchemy
  of mystical experiment!
How colourful Love's smile, at once
  gauge, flame and crucible inside
this universe of mind, inside
  the heart of our eternity.

Breakthrough

  If I could be the eye
    of wind to see the world
  or feel within a flame
    to purify the soiled!

  If I could break in waves
    of universal sound
  or energise the atom-heart
    with only light around!

  Please can I more and more
    approach the central core,
  in dying thus become the love
    that is You, Very Lord!

A child of the starry heaven
   lotus-postured meditates; drifts
of thought have all dissolved away;
   metamorphosis of knowledge
now illuminates each facet
   of perception into brilliance.

An atmosphere of music drives
   across creation's sky; swept on waves
of understanding he is drawn
   to expanding light; thunder from
the inner ocean speeds him
   surfing towards an endless shore.

On streams of truth he enters
   ancient symmetries of wisdom
where his sacred heart is lifted
   from the logic of base earth
and whirled in symphonies of fire
   to free dimensions of the air.

Bells at Trumpington Church

suddenly began to ring as Marianne, Lily and
James went to lay flowers on the tomb of
Gran and Grandad (25-4-2019).

Bells of joy rang out
on greeting Gran and Grandad
at their tomb.
This is the kind of love
they always dreamed of -
the embrace
of happy family.

The Call

If you want Goodness, Beauty, Truth
  you tread the Path. There burns a flame
cooler than the devil's game, its ardour
  and devotion unify

each slugged-out dialectic duel
  and prick the bubble politic.
Mind's bullet aimed for Goodness, fired,
  becomes the marksman, flying higher.

Through liquid lighter into gas
  the flame of love cremates all mass.
Rise up! Fall to the tug, the wish,
  call unremittingly to bring the bliss

of affluent and essential state
  whose orator is just a smile,
whose policy's to reconcile -
  come together, come to Prayer, Peace.

On a Broadcast Live from Mir (Peace)
Satellite to BBC, London, Christmas 1988

A peaceful eye surveys our ark
   from heaven. Unhastening sphere, the Earth
revolves through nothing, spins through wave
   on wave of life - womb, carrier, tomb,
our one and only hope and home.
   No boundary, no politics;

the sapphire waters, swirling clouds
   and land are granted us in trust.
Strip desire and burning as a candle-flame
   in 'Mir' treat Mother and her brood;
lead life as gently as you can,
   leave the planet spotless as you came.

The author has recently written a few more books (available from Amazon, Foyles, Waterstones, Barnes & Noble etc. and see website addresses on p.2):

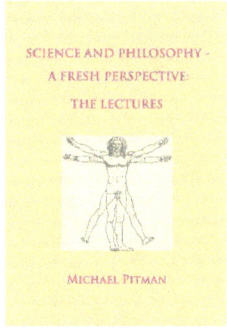
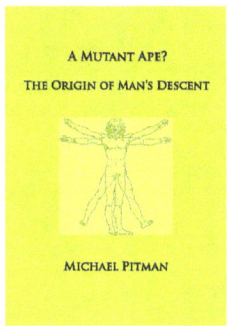
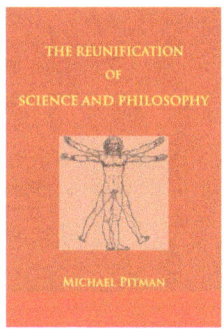

Image Credits:

Blue Marble / Our Ark: public domain; Wikimedia commons: *NASA* (1972)
Back cover: Asiatic Lily II, © David J. Bookbinder, flowermandalas.org